# Journey to Financial Freedom

Darlene Nuñez

# CONTENTS

# Acknowledgments

Many helped to make this book a reality. Having a great support system is why I have made it this far. I am blessed.

My heartfelt gratitude goes to my husband, Jose Rivera. The love, patience, and support you have provided for me to meet my goals and achieve my dreams genuinely amaze me. Thank you for believing in me!

My daughters, Kianny and Arianna Rivera, the level of understanding you have at your young age is beyond your years. Thank you for being patient with us during this time and for loving us unconditionally.

Miriam Morales, my incredible mother, thank you for being there for me along my journey. Your support and encouragement have helped me to accomplish many things in life. Thank you for raising me to believe I could achieve anything.

Loida Perez, my mother-in-law, you have loved me as one of your own, and for this, I feel like the luckiest woman in the world. You have been a therapist, a friend, and a mother. I hope to do half as good a job as what you have done for me, once I become a mother-in-law.

To my editor, Erica Anderson Thomas, you are absolutely amazing. Your insight and ideas on this book have been invaluable. I am eternally grateful for your wisdom and efforts in helping me get my message out.

To our friends & family for your understanding and support

through the times we had to say "no."

To all of my coaches and mentors who relentlessly worked with me to reach new heights, I am eternally grateful.

To our amazing clients: We are fortunate to work with each of you. We strive to continue to cultivate our business relationships and cherish every opportunity to serve and support you.

To my former bosses and coworkers who have influenced my life, you all inspire me in some way to become better, and for that, I thank you.

*Please visit my website at www.darlenenunezllc.com for updates and free resources*

# Introduction

As I write this, I ask myself whether I will be able to help my community, friends, family and others who will read this book. My way of thinking has changed drastically over the years. I am eager to share with you my wins and my struggles as well as my motivation and the inspiration to keep moving forward. More importantly, I'm excited to share how I, along with my husband, worked to achieve a better future for our family after surviving a major financial crisis. Despite the challenges and pitfalls, there were some necessary steps to living a more abundant and meaningful life.

I pray and cried many nights asking God if the solution was for me to join the military. As a middle schooler in Rio Rancho, New Mexico, I was part of the Junior Reserve Officer Training Corp. Later during my high school years in Puerto Rico, I was part of the Civil Air Patrol in Punta Salinas, and I loved it. I was passionate about going to the military and embraced that it was a real possibility for me. Although I prayed and cried about the decision, the reality was that my circumstances didn't allow for me to join. It hit me hard. I was surrounded by active duty soldiers, their wives, my military family and many coworkers who were living a decent life as a result of their employment with the government. It had a significant impact on my belief in achieving success.

Although I was driven by the security of being in the military, my career path led me on a journey that taught me many things about money management and financial education. In this book, I'm excited to share that journey with you. From the highs and lows to the mistakes and victories, I'm here to share the things that became building blocks in my life for financial success. I know that the golden nuggets I share are going to be of great benefit to you.

# Growing Up

During my childhood, my mom, dad, and Grandma Fela were a part of the village that took care of me. I was pretty much an average kid. My Grandma Fela in particular, helped my mom raise me from when I was just one month old. She gave me the knowledge of Jesus Christ at an early age, which was a blessing to me. During my teens, I was an honor student who loved dancing, especially in front of an audience. I had started dancing on stage at the age of five. If you ask any of my childhood friends who Darlene was, they would tell you that I was "the dancer." To this day, I always get teary eyed when I watch a great performance because although I never did this as an adult, I still experienced those great dancing moments during my childhood. The stage was my thing, and I still love dreaming of that feeling. Sadly, I don't have pictures or recordings of my performances, and I feel like I lost my beat a long time ago. The only way I could go back to dancing is with a lot of training. It would be amazing if I could train with Tricia Miranda, one of the greatest choreographers of today. A girl can dream…I *am* a fast learner!

It was in January of 1994 that my life changed drastically. I was 12 years old, and I had no idea of the new "adventure" I was about to start, far away from the place I called home. My parents separated, and I ended up living with my mom and her boyfriend. Before my parents were divorced, my mom was a professional working at Dupont Pharmaceutical. After the divorce, she became a stay-at-home mom. Everything seemed to happen so fast. We lost everything. I, a girl from the beautiful island of Puerto Rico, ended up starting middle school in Rio Rancho, New Mexico. This was where my mom decided to relocate with her boyfriend, to whom she had now become engaged.

Although our new life was on the mainland, I felt like I was on another planet. The music was entirely different. I was accustomed to Spanish music, but Mexican was the new normal. The school fashion trends were different and overall everything was strange and new to me. It wasn't all bad though. I did have the opportunity to speak more English in school. I visited the Sandia Mountain, saw hot air balloons for the first time, and I heard many stories about the Roswell

UFO incident back in the forties, as well as Area 51. Looking at the sky at night was always a fun adventure, and I also had the chance to see many Native Americans and their lovely adobe houses. Not to mention, as a Hispanic in New Mexico, I started watching *The Johnny Canales Show*. I became a fan of Selena when she was still alive, and also Queen Latifah. Do you remember when the big hit, "U.N.I.T.Y" came out? Or when wearing a key as a necklace pendant was super cool?

Although I have many good memories, some of them were traumatic. I will describe to you what I lived during those long 16 months in the States. When we first arrived in New Mexico, we started living with the brother of my mom's husband. Then we moved to live with his sister and her family. I felt as though we were homeless and I had no way to communicate with my family back in Puerto Rico. Shortly after, my stepdad rented a two bedroom house. It felt good to finally have a bedroom even if I was sharing it with my two little brothers. We slept on the floor in sleeping bags until my stepdad decided to rent some furniture. He finally found a job, but the weird thing was that we had to go with him and sit in the car all day, waiting for him to get off. What man on this planet makes his wife wait in the car with three kids for an entire eight-hour shift?! Only a person who is possessive. I came to see that this man was a complete monster.

He couldn't hold a job for long so guess what happened next? First, our furniture got repossessed since he was not making the payments. Then we were evicted from the house.

We were a family of five with nowhere to live, in a new

state, basically with no family. It was clear that his siblings did not want us back at their houses. Ultimately, a pastor allowed us to live at their old church location. It was a commercial building in a plaza with a bathroom but no shower or kitchen. I remember trying to take a bath at the sink. During this time we would request food from a local Women, Infant and Children food center, which was a short walk away. After some time, a really nice church member who was from the Philippines sheltered us for a couple of weeks.

After eight short months, we moved to Orlando, Florida. I remember the day we arrived in Orlando and drove past the Wet & Wild Water Park. I dreamt of going one day. I also remember my mom's husband taking me to a pawn shop to pawn my custom gold necklace. The necklace was etched with my name, and my mom had given it to me as a gift a few years prior. However, I really wanted to eat McDonald's instead of the salty crackers with cheese we had during the road trip. The $15 he received for my necklace were my only option to be able to afford a burger.

While we were in Florida between 1994 and 1995, I first went to Jackson Middle School then Glenridge Middle School in Winter Park. My mom's husband started working for apartment complexes doing woodwork in exchange for housing, so that worked out well for us. They did continue to struggle to get food on the table, but overall we were living a little better than we did in New Mexico. Although I was happy to see many Hispanics in this new state, I was ecstatic when my mom decided to go back to my little island eight months later. The decision was great, but she was now expecting a baby girl.

There was a drastic difference in our lives at this time. My mom formerly had a great career, drove a car with a cell phone in it, owned a beautiful home with central air in Puerto Rico, dressed professionally every day, and attended awesome events like Christmas parties. She was now living on Section 8, had no transportation, no job, and little money to spend. It was devastating. As a teenager, it was a tough experience coming back to my hometown but living at a different level. We went from having the best cars and clothes when my parents were together, to being a family on welfare in less than two years.

After going back to Puerto Rico, I was never the same. I wanted to listen to music in English, and I was desperately looking for my own identity. Most of the time I was dressing like Queen Latifah, with big pants, big shirts, and bandanas. I knew everyone when I came back except this girl named Lea. She wore the same style of clothes as me, so I knew that she came from the States. We had an instant connection and became best friends. Lea was born and raised on a military base in Virginia. Her parents had been deployed to Puerto Rico at the time.

It was in this period of my life when I became a rebel. I was determined to live somewhere other than with my mom and her husband. I would find ways not to go home, stay at other people's house or ask to go out but return very late at night. I did not want to see my stepdad's face. I had a lot of anger towards him. I felt that he had ruined my family. He was the reason my mom and dad were not together, although I knew deep in my heart that my parent's relationship was not going well way before this guy came into our lives. I still remember times when he would put a chain with a lock on the only exit to the house so that no one could leave while he was gone. His fear of my mom leaving him was so intense that he would lock us up in our own home. In my eyes, his behavior and actions were unacceptable.

At one point, my Grandma Fela asked my mom to allow me to attend a youth retreat at church. I knew almost everyone at the church since Grandma took me to church most Sundays. I was super excited to go and see some of my friends. Grandma Fela's daughter-in-law would be attending the retreat as well. She had known me since I was a little girl. Attending the retreat with her would make the weekend getaway even better because she was always fun to be with.

It was at this retreat that I accepted Jesus as my Savior. I surrendered, and I understood what it was to feel the presence of my Almighty God at 14 years old. I did not become perfect as a result of my salvation, but I did become a strong person of faith. My attitude finally took a turn for the better. I know that many people have painful experiences throughout life. These experiences can cause different types of damage to us. Sometimes we react in bad ways, but I can tell you from my own experiences that the best way to deal with these situations is to learn from them and to strive to move forward in every step you take.

I was so happy when my mom was approved to receive government assistance. The government helped us by providing housing. At this point, her husband was out of the picture for good. It was now just my mom, my two brothers, my little sister and me, the oldest. I felt like God was finally listening to my prayers, although I knew He was there the entire time. It is frustrating being stuck in a toxic relationship because you can't afford to move out with your children. Because of my mother's experience, I learned at a very young age to work hard and not to depend on a man for anything. My entire life has been inspired by the time my mom was with this person. These experiences gave me the motivation to keep moving forward. I remain consistent with accomplishing my goals because I have lived on the streets. I don't want to live that way ever again, nor do I want my kids to experience that.

During high school, we lived in a Section 8 duplex in Puerto Rico. My mom didn't have a car, so she walked everywhere she needed to go; even to pay the rent. She would work a couple of side hustles each month to make the money she needed. It was clear that my mom was trying her best to start a new life without her husband in the picture. She finally filed for divorce after months of separation. The best thing out of her relationship with him was the birth of my little sister.

When I entered high school in Levittown, Puerto Rico, I told one of my friends that my dream was to travel and own hotels. My thoughts reflected the experience of my recent travels to New Mexico and Florida. This friend was a senior in high school and suggested that I go into a program called Hospitality and Tourism. The program gave me the opportunity to travel during the summer to Johnson & Wales University in Rhode Island. I participated in an English immersion program and also considered going to the college after I graduated. During the program, I worked in a respectable hotel as a housekeeper. I was really excited! This was a great stepping stone and a big deal for me. Inside, I knew I would become the owner of the hotel soon. "Darlene the Dreamer" was starting to rise. Little did I know that my dreams and goals would change at every step I took over the course of my life. One thing I learned very quickly was that working in the hospitality industry does not equate to being a tourist. Of course, I was thinking it was going to be a travel adventure. At 16 years old, I had it all wrong. Working in the hospitality industry means that you work most days when other people are off. On the island, Christmas time is full of what we call snowbirds, and it requires us to work more.

While working at the Intercontinental Hotel in Isla Verde, I met Jose, the love of my life. Jose would do things for me secretly. My friends and I worked part-time as housekeepers. Sometimes as I would go through the line at lunchtime, a cafeteria worker would hand me a special dessert. It was usually chocolate covered strawberries. I knew I had a secret admirer at my job, but initially, I did not know who it was. I was so naïve that I thought someone was playing a joke on me. I mean, all of my friends were pretty. Why me? With the help of some of my friends, he finally dared to tell me. We dated for months, and he went to my high school graduation in 1999. Shortly after, I started attending Sagrado Corazon University in Puerto Rico. Ultimately, I moved from home to live with Jose and his family in another town in Puerto Rico called Loiza.

I loved the Loiza community for keeping the older traditions of our Puerto Rican culture alive. I especially loved Sundays during bomba nights. Everyone was friendly, and they loved enjoying time with neighbors, family, and friends. My mother-in-law is from this town, and I was amazed to meet someone who was so much like my Grandma Fela. They were both always reading their bibles, worshipping while cooking or cleaning, and giving advice according to the scriptures. I also discovered that Loiza is populated by the largest community of African descendants on the island of Puerto Rico. I will always cherish my experience living there.

# Eighteen & Pregnant

Jose purchased a new car and taught me how to drive. I was able to continue my college attendance with the help of Pell Grants and student loans. It was after seven short months of living together that I became pregnant with our first child. Here I was at the age of 18 pregnant and not even two semesters into college. I was happy, scared, and confused among other things.

The feeling of freedom after I graduated high school gave me the notion that it was time for me to create my future. Sometimes I look back and wonder why I wanted to grow up so fast. I only wish I had planned better for my post-high school life.

I ended up quitting my job while I was pregnant. I felt like I had no clue what I wanted to accomplish. I realized that having a baby on the way can quickly change your path. I suffered a lot while I was pregnant. Although I had people around who cared about me, I was missing my siblings and my mom. Also, my boyfriend was working the night shift at the hotel. He would often hang out with friends after work and would get home very late or sometimes the next morning. I was living a total nightmare during those days because I felt like I didn't know if he really wanted to be with me. When I had Kianny in January of 2001, we were thrilled. We wanted to give her the best as all parents do. I went back to work and college six months after she was born.

I returned to work as a hostess at a restaurant in the San Juan Hotel called Veranda. There was also a rooftop restaurant called The Ranch that was frequented by many famous people. I once saw Donatella Versace with many bodyguards by the pool. I went on to see many others who were well known in the music industry. It was awesome to see so many celebrities, but I realized that the Tourism industry was full of managers who had their positions because of their years of experience. I was going to college for it. I decided I did not want to go to school for four years only to end up in competition with people who had experience without a degree. Two years into my degree in Tourism, I decided to quit.

My mom had moved back to Florida while I was pregnant. She got married for a third time to an active duty Army soldier. He was a friend from her childhood years in her hometown back in New York. After Kianny was born, she offered to let me live with her until I could get settled, but the 9/11 catastrophe postponed my plans to move. I waited almost a year and got fed up with Jose's behavior. He continued to party and hang out all night. I never knew whether he was coming home and dealt with so many tears, feelings of regret, anger, hate and so many other things. It reminded me of how much my mom suffered with her ex-husband as a result of his jealousy. Although this wasn't my experience, it was just devastating for me to be with a guy who did not care to come home after work. I had enough, so I told him I was leaving.

Moving day finally came. I had packed my things, and the moving boxes were ready to be shipped to Florida. At one point while we were packing, I remember telling my boyfriend not to pack his things if he was not going with me. He had said that he was going with me, but I couldn't trust those words. He did not get an airplane ticket, advising me to go ahead and that he would follow me later. I left with baby Kianny at the beginning of August in 2002. I was 20 years old and ready to start a new life. I lived with my mom and new stepdad for two months. My stepdad was serving in Orlando on active duty at the time, and I was able to take advantage of that extra help.

Just a few days before I turned 21, I got my Florida driver's license. I was so excited but had become fearful that Jose was not going to move to the States as he had said. I knew it was going to be hard for him to leave his seven-year position at the hotel because that's what he loved to do. To my surprise, the day came when he finally arrived. It was a little less than 30 days after my arrival. We both went to job interviews right away, as we knew we needed to get started building our future and our lives as a family. At that time, the infamous Mall at Millenia was opening, so we both went to interviews at restaurants there. Jose was hired at The Cheesecake Factory as a busboy, and I started at P.F. Chang's as a food runner. It was no surprise that we did not get server positions because our English was not so great. However, we both started working, and that was our primary goal.

I often see people being picky about choosing a job or even rejecting a job because it's not what they want. I understand having standards, but if you are new to an area or don't speak the native language, get the first job you can so you can get the experience. Work as though you are the owner of that company. If you decide later on that the job is not for you, then go ahead and start looking for something else. I have also realized how important it is to always learn as much as possible when on a job. I learned to observe not only my duties but the supervisor, manager, and business owner. I ask myself whether I want to be in their position if I continue working there. That's the mindset I developed when I was younger, and it has served me well in each position I have attained.

I was terrible as a food runner, so I lasted a couple of months. My mom had recently given birth to baby number five and was ready to become a stay-at-home mom. She immediately referred me to an open position at her federal job, a local Navy Exchange Store. I was hired and worked for some time as a retail associate. At that time I was selling crystals, figurines, vacuums, and jewelry, among other things, at the Navy Exchange Store. I met some of the most amazing people there. Shortly after my life was getting better, I was involved in a hit and run car accident. After whoever was driving left the scene, I was waiting for the cops in the rain for nearly an hour before I was able to file a report. While I was waiting, an older lady pulled up with damage to her vehicle. There was white paint on her car. My best guess is that the vehicle that hit my car caused damage to her car too. This lady left in an ambulance to go the hospital. My car was totaled, but it was clear that I was not responsible for what happened to her car since my car was red and the paint from the damage on her car was white. Little did I know that this would ultimately have a devastating effect on my life.

We moved to a two bedroom apartment, but we were struggling. We only had one car and had to start paying for daycare as a result of my mom and her husband relocating to Germany. We didn't have any emergency funds at all and were living paycheck to paycheck. Our car was old and wasn't very reliable. It went out of commission many times because of mechanical issues.

I had a good friend and co-worker from The Netherlands who was retiring. She was a sweet soul and allowed me to use her car sometimes to get my baby girl from daycare or take Jose to work. Sometimes I would pick her up at work, and she would drive me home. She would rather let me borrow her car than to let it sit in the parking lot while she was working. I will always remember her generosity because I knew no one else was willing to do that, especially with the traffic laws here in Florida. She was an angel to our family in our most difficult times.

With no immediate family present, we had no motivation to celebrate the holidays. I vividly remember the first Christmas in Florida with Jose and the baby. We did not get a Christmas tree or decorations, and we couldn't afford to buy new clothes for winter. I am most sure God put my friend from The Netherlands in our lives for a reason. She came to me at work and gave me a $100 gift card from Sears. She said it was for me to go shopping with my family at the mall. I couldn't believe it! With that gift card, she made my first Christmas in Florida. It was such a memorable thing.

In 2004, Jose and I decided to get married officially. We wanted God to bless our marriage, and she was there to witness us tying the knot. She coordinated the reception at Chili's Restaurant with the rest of our team from work. Now, I'm sure some would ask, "Who would do a wedding reception at Chili's?!" Me! It was economical for Jose and me, as everyone paid their own bill. There was no mess to clean, and it was a lot of fun spending time with my coworkers. It was the best reception ever! I am genuinely grateful to God for putting her and this incredible team in my life.

This was a lesson to be grateful for the people who are helping you along the way. It could be someone who enables you to take care of your kids while you go to school or someone who gives you a ride to work or even someone who offers you a great opportunity. I have always believed that it is no coincidence that God surrounds us with these people.

After a year in Florida, Jose found a position at a great corporation as a driver. The pay and schedule were much better than it was as a busboy, so our lives started to get a little better. We were still struggling with transportation. I had a co-worker who gifted us an old but reliable car. People at my job took me under their wings as they got acquainted with me, my situation and my struggles. I was 21 years old when I started working there. Many of the other women were older and married to active duty soldiers or veterans, working just to get out of the house. They had the financial stability I needed, but I was far from it at that time.

I developed a friendship with an amazing co-worker who was from Korea. I will always remember her telling me to give myself four years to get better situated. At the time, she was a real estate investor and said to me that she bought properties anywhere her husband was stationed. I was always excited to talk to her because she was a savvy woman. Marsy was another lady that gave me a piece of advice I will never forget. She was a mature lady, probably in her 60's at that time. She would tell me, "Don't stay here forever. Go out there, get prepared and get a better job." Almost every week, she would also say, "Don't be like me, I've been working here too long!" Some people would hear those ladies and ignore their advice, but not me. I paid close attention to every single word. All these ladies in some way or another empowered me to invest in self-development and to help others. Because of my interaction with them, I started to want more out of life.

# Learning to Make a Living

I started an ESOL program at Valencia Community College. I went there for two long years. I didn't get a degree, but I completed a course to improve my ability to speak English. I sacrificed time with my family four nights every week for two years, but it was well worth it. Have you ever heard the saying, "Do what others won't so later you could do what others can't"? I love that saying, and there is so much truth to it. Sacrifice for a period and see the reward later. It may not be a huge stepping stone for most, but for me, it was the beginning of a better life, a better career and many opportunities to come.

The Hurricane season in 2004 was a disaster in Central

Florida. Four hurricanes came back to back, and many places were damaged including the site where I was working. My hours were cut so I decided to get a part-time job at UPS loading trucks at night. With this schedule, I did not have to pay the high daycare fees for my little one. Taking care of her in the morning was my primary goal. I worked from 11 pm till 4 am for a couple of months. I quickly realized that I was too tired in the morning hours to take care of my daughter, so that did not work out.

During this time I started researching how to purchase real estate. I was tired of renting. It was always a dream of mine, and I wanted to buy a house for my family. I found out that I first needed to contact a loan officer at a bank or a mortgage broker. Well, instead of me finding one, I decided to become one. In 2005, I started taking weekend classes to become a loan officer. It was pretty simple back then, just before the messy Housing Crash. As I was finishing the course, I was offered a position as a loan officer at a local mortgage lending firm. The money was significant but only if you were able to keep a pipeline. I would sometimes go weeks and months without a paycheck because it was 100% commission based. But I was just grateful that I finally had an office job. I remember seeing the top producers and paying attention to what they were doing. They were doing things like going to investor's meetings and having lunch with clients. It was a fantastic atmosphere. I was a part of the rookies who mostly did cold calling, which was not fun at all, but I was learning the business, and I was okay with that. I did make a considerable amount of money, even if it was inconsistent.

I realized my dream of becoming a homeowner at the age of 24. I purchased my mom's house since we were already renting it, and we were all so happy. This milestone was one of my best and worst moves. Let me explain why.

Remember that car accident I mentioned from 2003? Well, it came back up. I don't know whether the attorney saw that I acquired an asset or if the statute of limitations was approaching, but in 2006 I received a summons to which I had no clue how to respond. The old lady ended up suing me for around $28,000. I remember crying and not knowing what to do. I quickly called my mom, and she advised me to ignore it. I had no money in the bank so my mom figured they couldn't get anything from me. My stepdad was the owner of the car I was driving that day, so he was also in a mess. However, he was quickly exonerated because he was deployed at the time of the accident. The main problem was that the car was not insured at the time of the crash, so I was fully liable for any damages although this lady just appeared at my accident site minutes before the cops arrived.

I truly believe this lady was a scam artist. I ended up suffering for this for many years including cancellation of my driver license, high insurance premiums, reports to my public record, denial of great job opportunities and so on. I now understand the importance of having auto insurance. It's also important to not ignore any legal correspondence. Ask for a settlement out of court if possible. Always get legal advice immediately, and of course, have an emergency fund in place at all times.

I approached my boss at the mortgage office when I received the summons, and he gave me a piece of advice. He said, "Whatever you wanted to get before this, get it now. Your credit will be ruined for a long time."

I quickly lost sight of my real estate dreams and dreaded the possibility of my financial future being ruined long-term. I was not having it. I told my husband to get the cars we always wanted. We financed both a nice Lincoln SUV and a Cadillac CTS. They were both used but in excellent condition. Not long after that, I realized that the car payments were a big chunk of our income. I could no longer work by commission only. I wanted to get a regular 40 hour per week job with consistent pay so I could pay for my house and cars. Kianny entered kindergarten around this time. I went through a staffing agency, and I interviewed for a receptionist position at a local real estate builder's office. How awesome was that? I was excited to get that job! They were Cubans just like my prior boss at the mortgage firm.

I learned so much in spite of being a receptionist. I knew I was working for someone exceptional. My boss had come from Cuba many years prior and worked his tail off to become a great home builder. I admired his family business. I noticed that they were very supportive of one another and were a close-knit family. They also gave back to the community by working with different charities.

I was given a tour of a new subdivision they had completed. I cried. I had developed a passion for real estate, and it was fascinating to see other Latinos doing big things in the industry. During my time with the company, I was able to meet and speak with the mayor of Orlando. I also had the opportunity to get acquainted with a fellow Puerto Rican woman who had become a home builder. It was imperative to me to do great at this job. Little did they know that I desired to keep moving up within the company. I remember telling one of my coworkers (who happened to be the owner's niece) that I wanted to keep that job forever. She responded that I had to want more out of life. I had to have goals. I proactively took her advice and decided it was time for me to go back to college. I decided to major in Accounting. I was inspired by both the accountant and the staff accountant at the company. My financial situation also inspired me. I had two car payments, a house to pay for and no personal finance education. Honestly, I was still confused about what major to take. Although my main dream as a high schooler was to become a real estate entrepreneur (own hotels and houses), I did not want to major in Business Administration because I did not want to waste money on a degree that was too broad. Many could get positions without it. Competing in corporate America with people who didn't have a degree was not what I had in mind. I did not want to waste my money on college.

Later in the year, I asked my boss for a piece of advice regarding mortgages. I wanted to know whether I should refinance my house and pay off my debt. He told me that I could, but people often end up getting into more debt. He advised me that it was ok, but to stay debt free after that. Those were such words of wisdom. Not long after that conversation, I was let go due to the recession of 2008. I was devastated, but I knew the economy was not doing well. Layoffs were unavoidable at that time.

During the time I was laid off, I began receiving unemployment benefits. I decided to use CareerBuilder to search for a new job. I applied for over 50 jobs each week and interviewed for many positions, to no avail. I became desperate. I was about to lose my house and cars. After some time, I realized that my previous work experience mainly utilized general administrative skills like answering phones and screening calls, customer service, sales and of course, Hospitality. I concluded that I needed to master a new skill. This was a wakeup call. I had come to the point of feeling like I wasn't going to get a job because I did not have enough education. It felt like people who seemed to have superpowers took the few jobs that were available.

I went to the unemployment office to inquire about any benefits I could receive during this time. To my surprise, one of them was a full scholarship for a tech program or trade school. I worked diligently to attend all the appointments that had been set for me to get started. I was appointed a counselor who helped me decide on a great career based on the job market at the time. I received a voucher to pay for the trade school. I took full advantage of the opportunity and started going to Winter Park Tech during the day. At night I was attending college classes for my Accounting Degree at the University of Turabo, at the Metro Orlando Campus. I discovered that I love working with numbers and analyzing them even better.

In the meantime, my husband was also laid off from his management position at Sherwin Williams. He was able to find another job in the field that same year, but it was entry level. He decided to start his own painting business on the side. He kept his position until the painting business was generating more revenue. I met many people like Jose and I.

These were people who realized that only having a job didn't provide the stability that was needed, and decided to start their own business. People who chose to go to school while receiving unemployment benefits to reinvent themselves. I believe that the actions we took helped us to build a foundation for success.

In my tech school program, I was the only person in my group who decided to do an internship. This was during the summer of 2009. Doing an internship was not required to graduate, but my teacher advised me to do it. She explained that it would get my feet in the door within the field and gain some experience. My instructor was aware that I was in the process of losing everything. I confided in her when I was still undecided about starting school and continued applying for jobs so I wouldn't lose my things. She would call and email me to provide encouragement. She knew better than I did that this would turn out to be a great opportunity. She was right. I will always be grateful for having such a great instructor.

Once I finished the class, I contacted several of my friends to see if they had any connections to a medical office so that I could get my internship done. I vividly remember speaking to a co-worker who was a good friend at my previous home builder's job. She gave me the name of a medical office and told me to go there and ask for a specific nurse. It was this connection that allowed me to get into the medical field doing billing and coding. It turned out to be a great career. Because of her referral, I was able to enter the field a little bit quicker. It's not easy to get started as a Medical Biller & Coder. Most offices require some level of experience before hiring someone. That referral provided tremendous help.

Once I completed my internship, I was hired shortly after at a medical office in downtown Orlando. I learned about many different things including Medicare Risk, Adjustments, Denials, and Credentials. I especially enjoyed the location downtown. My office had a beautiful view, and a movie theater plaza was just a short elevator ride down from my floor. That location was a popular spot for local young professionals. During lunchtime, you could see the executives walking the downtown streets and I even sometimes felt like a high executive working there because of the atmosphere. Everything went well most of the time, but I recall overhearing other employees discussing their salaries during lunch breaks. I knew this was something no one should be talking about. They would continuously talk about the wages that were being paid to office managers, nurses, doctors or other clerks. It just felt very unprofessional, especially the information that was being leaked from the Accounting staff. Accounting was my college major, so I knew this was not right.

Soon after, I was hired by a major hospital. I felt great about it although the lunch break was only 30 minutes and now I had to wear a uniform. Having to scarf down my lunch every day quickly became a big disappointment. I went from feeling like an executive to working in a cubicle in an old office space. I did my best not to complain.

My primary focus was to keep a salary coming in and to improve my skills. My number one goal was to stay employable. I couldn't forget having to survive on those unemployment checks which were $275 a week. That was a catastrophic $6.22 per hour! This maximum amount per week is still the same, nearly ten years later! Florida ranks as one of the lowest-paying states in the nation when it comes to unemployment.

Although we were making strides to increase our income, we had gotten too far behind on all of our bills. We decided to file for bankruptcy in 2010. I was devastated. I felt like a complete loser. Although I knew that millions were going through this at the same time, there is no feeling like realizing you have hit rock bottom. This time in the U.S. Economy was referred to as the Great Recession. Banks were taking forever to foreclose on properties, so that gave us some time to save for a deposit so we could move. It was devastating to leave our house after eight years primarily because it was my mom's house. I have to admit that it was a relief to finally leave because the bank was going to auction off the property in a short amount of time.

During this time my family did not understand what was going on in the U.S. since some were living overseas and others on military bases. It was hard for me to explain our financial situation to any of them. I felt like I didn't have anyone to talk to even though millions were going thru this same situation.

We decided to move to a good community with excellent schools in the area of Lake Nona, the infamous Medical City. The house we found was beautiful and spacious. We couldn't have been happier. I was so excited for 2011. I was determined that this was going to be "my year." I would be graduating with my Accounting degree during the summer, and my life was getting much better. Finally, I felt like my hard work was paying off. The key was that I decided to focus on getting educated during the recession. It was like the push I needed to improve my professional life.

# Material Things Are Not the Answer

My dad was a hardworking man who spent 35 years working for the police department in Puerto Rico. When he retired, he received less than $1,600 each month for his pension. He couldn't live off of this because it only covered his mortgage payment. He started working for the Puerto Rican Housing Administration to supplement his income. He was making an additional $1800 a month to survive, but he always seemed to struggle. My father's situation was a constant reminder that I don't want to work for 35 years, retire to then work again to have to cover a high mortgage payment or material things I cannot afford. Shortly after my terrible financial crisis, I realized that I did not need to impress anyone with my house, cars or clothes. On more than a few occasions, I suggested that he move to a smaller place.

Ultimately, my dad filed for a Chapter 7 bankruptcy. He put the house on his bankruptcy but was never served papers to move out. He lived day by day with the worry of losing his home. I told him about the situation with my bankruptcy and how I had to move when the bank was selling the house. My father continued to live on the property, and it was primarily because it previously belonged to his father. Can you imagine living each day waiting for someone to show up at your house to tell you that you need to move? My dad was stressed as a result of this situation, which exacerbated other health issues he had.

My dad ended up having an open heart surgery. Once he was released from the hospital, my amazing and caring Grandpa dropped him off at home. My understanding is that my Grandpa offered to help him, but my macho dad did not want any help. A couple of hours later, he drove himself to a supermarket to buy some groceries. When he came back home, he started cleaning, and that's how he was found a couple of days later. My dad had suffered a heart attack and died in his home just hours after being discharged. That meant he had no visitors for the day after he left the hospital. No one knew he had passed away. Because of the climate, his body had already started to decompose at the time he was found. My father had six children. Although I spent many years thinking about the beautiful house I could get for my dad, I realized that all he needed was for his children to be there for him. Whether it was for grocery shopping or helping him around the house for a few days, he just needed someone present with him. At the time he passed away, he only needed a helping hand and I nor any of my siblings were there. My dad passed away at 57 years old, a few weeks shy of my graduation.

I will always remember him for wanting great things, working hard and loving us unconditionally. In my heart, I know he deserved a better life than what he lived. My dream had always been to one day buy my dad a house. For many years, I dreamt of making it happen, but it didn't. I was like a lot of people, contemplating the day I would hit the lottery and be able to help him. The reality was, that was not what my father needed on his last day on Earth.

I am sharing this because my dad's situation helped me to realize that material things are not the answer. If losing my dad was a way of putting me in a position to share a message to help others understand this, his time on earth was not in vain. The reality is that helping others is not always easy. It can sometimes derail your schedule and cost you time, money and other resources. However, this is the best way to show your loved ones that they truly matter to you. If your parents are alive, spend time with them. I feel like I must emphasize this. Help them with errands, take them to their doctor's appointments or make a simple phone call every few days. That is what they need. Don't worry about giving them money, a house or a new car. They need to feel love, especially during times they need you the most.

A couple of months after my college graduation, I received some great news. First, I was hired permanently as a Coder for the hospital. Then, I found out I was pregnant with my second child. Although I was happy and considered it a blessing, I was scared. I had suffered and struggled so much during the first experience that it made me feel like I didn't want to have more children. Between the fact that we had no family to help at times to having low-income and a lack of medical insurance, it was a real sacrifice. It reminds me of the game Cashflow 101. No matter how much you have coming in, there is always something going out. Although I'm still happy to hear the news of a friend expecting, I worry. It was a mindset I developed after the struggle I had with my first child. I was sure it was going to be a repeat of that situation, but I was wrong.

Initially, I felt like I needed an SUV since I had a newborn on the way. I was able to finance a pre-owned SUV just a year after my bankruptcy. I took on another debt as a result of my "broke mentality." The reality was that I did not need a car payment. This only made it harder for me to stay home with the baby because I would have to work to pay for it. My husband, however, was doing well with his business. Life was a little more comfortable for us at this point. We decided to downsize to save more money before our baby came so shortly after, we moved to a townhome in the same area. When she finally arrived, we named our baby girl Arianna. Our home felt complete with so much love and joy.

A few weeks after Arianna was born, my husband started experiencing some depression. Because of this, he began to decline and was working less. Here I was, hoping to be able to stay home with the baby, but ended up having to work to make up for the income that wasn't being generated by my husband. It was not the first time my husband had dealt with depression, however, this time it was so unexpected. The first time he had this experience was during the recession. I understood entirely because it was a lot for the both of us. This time, we were in a completely different situation. We both had a steady income, and we were maintaining our lives pretty well.

Depression is strange, and I didn't understand it. It is a more significant problem in today's world than some want to admit, and it is something that we as a society should talk about more. Although it is difficult for some people to share, I am not ashamed of talking about what my husband and I went through. He would not interact with anyone and often stayed in bed. He ignored whatever was going on around the house, and even stopped answering the business calls. I was dealing with this all by myself. It was difficult coping with this because it wasn't clear to me why my husband was even depressed. I became furious. I couldn't believe my husband was letting go of everything after we just had our newborn. How was this possible? I tried to look for ways to continue thriving, even if that meant living in a less expensive place so we could afford everything on just my income. We had become a family of four that was counting on my salary alone.

My coworkers were not aware of the trouble I was dealing with at home this time. I suffered in silence at work each day, sometimes leaving my newborn with my husband knowing he was not doing well. Fortunately, he turned out to be a perfect dad and took care of baby Arianna better than anyone else could have. He also started extreme couponing to save money on regular household expenses.

# Live Below Your Means

A couple of months went by, and I started to hear rumors that my department was going to be eliminated. I decided to start an online search for new opportunities. I found a job with a higher salary that I could do from home. I felt like God heard my prayers! I was excited to be able to take care of my baby and generate income at the same time. I also found a house that had a Lease-Purchase option. It was in an inexpensive area in Casselberry, and we quickly took advantage of this deal. I went from paying $1,250 to $700 per month. With a higher salary and lower rent, we were progressing in a significant way. I learned a great lesson during this time, and that is to live below your means! The funny thing is that I didn't discover this as a result of the bankruptcy, I found this out as a result of our experience when my husband dealt with depression. If you have a two-income household, it is best to try living as much as possible on one income. It will lessen the burden if someone loses their job.

After we moved, my husband started to get back on his feet. I noticed that his depression was slowly going away as he stayed busy. He began working again, but initially, the jobs were not consistent, so he started making improvements to our new property. In time, we found a company that was looking for a Refinisher. My husband started working with this company as a subcontractor. This worked out perfectly for us because this eliminated the need for us to find clients for our business. My husband ended up doubling his income and ultimately closed our business to focus on working as a subcontractor. This was great because we no longer had the stress of managing a business. At the rate things were going, we were able to save some cash because we were intentional about living below our means. It made me wonder why we didn't think of this before.

Life continued to get progressively better. We were finally able to afford for Kianny, our older daughter, to participate in dance and volleyball. It was something she always desired to do. Kianny was very talented from the time she was very young. She loved dancing, fashion, modeling, and arts. People often had suggestions for classes to put her in, but some people around us started to criticize us for our ability to allow our girls to participate in extracurricular activities. It was sad to see some of the very people who were once supportive turn jealous. I would have expected for them to be happy for us, but unfortunately, they were not. I learned a crucial lesson in this, and that was to not allow the opinions of others to dictate my life. People will have an opinion of your life whether you do well or not. I decided to hold my head high and give my children great experiences and memories. These were priceless moments, and my husband and I had worked hard to get to that point.

# Money Mindset Change

Many people, including myself at one point, feel the need to live outside their means or "keep up with the Joneses." I have learned that there are more important things to consider and work towards such as having a peaceful home or life and working on your plans or your legacy. Have you thought about what will happen if you lost your job or other means of income? Do you have any resources in place if that happens? Or even worse, what would happen if you lost your life? What would your family do? Would they be able to manage financially without you here? These life events are unavoidable. The best thing you can do is to set yourself and your family up to have what you all would need in the event of these unfortunate events.

If you find yourself considering these things,

understand that the first step is to stop taking on more debt. Stop buckling under the pressure of comparison and pretending to have what you can't afford. One of the ways I was able to counter this was distancing myself from people who couldn't understand where my husband and I were on our journey. We had come to the point of not going out, creating budgets and eliminating spending on things we didn't need. We opted to put instant gratification aside and always think long-term. I knew I wanted assets that didn't depreciate. I realized that I had accepted having a car payment as a way of life. The reality is that I was sending my hard earned money to a bank every month. Money that I should have been investing in my family. It feels good now to drive an older car and have that extra money for my daughters to participate in their activities.

We ended up moving again after discovering we had a sex offender in our neighborhood. We were able to buy a new house with my mom's help. As our finances continued to improve, I decided to work on something else: My health. I had been working at a desk for years, and now as I was working from home, my weight continued to get worse. My work area was just a short distance from my kitchen, and for almost two years, I consistently worked overtime to increase my take-home pay. As a result of my eating habits and lack of being active, I had gained 30lbs in less than nine months. I started doing CrossFit, and it helped me to get into shape and regain my self-esteem. Once we got settled in our new house, I developed an exercise regimen. I worked out for a minimum of an hour each day. I would also walk daily. Mentally and physically I could feel myself getting stronger. I kept myself motivated on my weight loss journey by signing up for 5K races and mud runs. I participated in both a half marathon and a full marathon. I even started listening to audiobooks and podcasts as I worked out. I loved being able to multitask in that way.

Although things had gotten progressively better for me on a personal level, I was starting to feel that my husband was unhappy again. He started to complain about his job, and it quickly affected me. One night around 3:00 am, I woke up and had an anxiety attack. I was in tears. My husband inquired about what was wrong, and I told him I was never going to be able to pay off my student loans. I had only been making the minimum payment, but the balance wasn't decreasing. It was killing me inside. The stress of the student loans along with hearing my husband complain about his job made me fear the idea of struggling again. I wanted to continue moving forward. I felt like it was unacceptable at this point to go back to having a one income household. The reality was that I had to be honest with myself. My student loan debt was the result of the fact that I went to a private college and I took the maximum amount for my loans every semester. I used the loans to pay for school, but also for vacations, car payments, as well as house payments during the recession. I should have been aware of the fact that I was going to have to pay all of that money back. Using student loans for living expenses was a big mistake. Now I was dealing with the compound interest, which is a complete nightmare. People often say that student loans are good debt because you are "investing in yourself," but I think this is nonsense. The compound interest makes it difficult to pay the loans off. A great way to figure out how much you are paying in interest is to do this simple formula.

Here is a breakdown of compound interest calculated at 5.75% on a loan balance of $55,000:

| Interest/Loan Balance = Daily Rate | Daily Rate*30 = Monthly Compound Interest |
|---|---|
| 5.75% / $55,000 = $8.66 | $8.66 x 30 = $259.93 |

### $259.80 of interest in ONE MONTH!

In order for me to pay this down, I needed to make a payment of more than my minimum of $260 per month. There were some other things that I didn't realize about this particular debt. First, it is not dischargeable during bankruptcy. Filing for bankruptcy wiped out most of my obligations, but the student loans were not. Failure to pay federal loans can result in garnishment of both your tax returns and your paychecks. I decided to attack the principal balance for my student loans aggressively. My husband was in 100% support of my goal to accomplish paying them off. We worked as a team, and this was a key factor. I strongly encourage graduates to start paying off those debts as soon as possible after graduation, or even start paying while still in school, to avoid the long-term issues that come along with making the minimum payment. Also, do not upgrade your lifestyle after college if you know you have debt that needs to be tackled.

# Being an Entrepreneur

After some time, my husband decided he wanted to start his company again. Although I was happy that he wanted to do this, I was in a panic because I didn't want him to fall into depression again. Entrepreneurship is great, but it takes a lot of hard work to build a company. I was apprehensive, but I still wanted to support my husband. I did that by researching how to market the opportunity so that we could build our clientele. We were aware of some of the things his former boss did to get clients, so we tried some of those methods. As a result of the things we learned and executed, we were able to gain a reasonable number of clients within three months of relaunching the business. We used multiple platforms and leveraged social media as a part of our plan. This along with my husband's excellent work ethic is what made things come together.

We along with our family and friends were prayerful about relaunching the business. As people of faith, we didn't want to take those steps without consulting the Lord. I remember my mother-in-law telling me not to worry about the company because it didn't belong to us. She encouraged me to see it as the Lord's company, and myself and my husband as the stewards who were ordained to manage it. I was relieved at being able to take on this perspective. It helped me to control my negative thoughts, and I felt more confident in acknowledging that God was in control of this venture.

During this time, I secretly applied to the University of Central Florida to see if I would get accepted, and I was. I was excited but scared at the same time. I thought that because we were doing well financially, that it would be a good idea to pursue my Master's degree. This would put my student loans in deferment, and I wouldn't have to make any payments. My husband did NOT think this was a good idea. The reality is that going back to school was a shot in the dark. I was going to pursue another degree with no plan for how I was going to utilize it. I already had my Bachelor's in Accounting and I wasn't using it. I was still making a decent salary based on the knowledge I gained during trade school. I knew that having a Master's would open more doors of opportunity, but I did not need to increase my student loan debt. I was contemplating ways to pause or to get the student loans forgiven with no luck.

The idea of going into the military resurfaced. It was now 13 years from the previous time I had considered it, and

I was not only more physically fit, but there were also benefits like Student Loan Repayment that would be a tremendous help. I trained consistently to make sure I met the fitness requirements, but when I went to the recruiter's office, they told me to lose another ten pounds. I was also advised that the Student Loan Repayment incentive was no longer offered.

I was disappointed, but I forged forward to lose those ten pounds. It seemed that those were the hardest ten pounds to lose. My motivation declined more and more as the news settled within me of the Student Loan Repayment program not being offered. I realized that going to the military was not a dream I wanted to fulfill. I had allowed this idea that going to the military was a surefire way to get out of debt and live a prosperous life. For years I had been fed that federal employment is the way to go because of lifetime benefits such as the pension and health insurance. Military soldiers gain leadership skills and earn the respect of society which are other benefits of joining the armed forces. For years, I observed as family and friends joined the military, retired then enjoyed the perks of the military life. Secretly, I felt inadequate. Although Jose and I were educated, had excellent skills, and possessed that entrepreneurial spirit, not having government jobs just made me feel like we weren't "good enough." I was tired of comparing our life to the lives of those who were around us. I let go of the idea that being in the military was necessary and shifted my priorities.

As a result of comparing my life to those around me, I realized that I was being ungrateful. I could feel God showing me that over and over again. He had been guiding me all this time, giving me the wisdom to see far more than what I could see on my own. I decided to make a list of the things for which I was grateful. It started with my ability to work from home, having a flexible schedule, having a successful business, having healthy children to having a new house, food in our refrigerator, unconditional love from my husband, and so many other things. I realized that this list was *endless*. I realized that I am blessed beyond measure. I came to the point of realizing that I needed to take responsibility for my actions and stay focused on the things I had been doing to achieve the level of success we had attained.

# Overcoming Financial Stress

Getting prepared for retirement became a priority since I knew getting a pension was out of the question. I finally realized that my entrepreneurial spirit was much stronger than I knew and that I could create wealth for myself. I knew that I did not have to work a nine to five my entire life, and that I needed to start preparing for retirement. I didn't want to wait until I was in my 60's to only receive Social Security benefits.

Within two years, we were able to pay off everything except our home and the student loans. Cars payments, credit cards, personal loans, medical bills and IRS bills were gone. We even shifted the extracurricular activities that our

48

daughters were involved in so that it was more cost-effective. For example, we had Kianny try out for the school volleyball team rather than have her on a local private team. We did everything from utilizing colorful "debt free" charts and spreadsheets to creating calendars with the numbers so that we would have a visual representation of our progress. Sometimes we felt burned out, but it was a fun journey that gave us beautiful results.

Because our mortgage was a significant expense, I requested for the bank to take out our PMI, or Private Mortgage Insurance because the house had increased in value. I was able to free up $250 per month by doing this. We had insurance in place for everything. I felt less fear and panic because I felt prepared. There is no feeling like not having financial stress. Having an emergency fund was an essential part of that financial stability as well. This was cash we had tucked away that was ready in case we had an emergency or unexpected expense. Trust me, when you have $500 to $1000 saved and you get a flat tire, you'll be relieved at having that cash on hand for the replacement versus charging it to a credit card.

# Things to Remember

## Kid's Education

More than likely our daughters will attend college. We did not save anything over the course of the years since I am still paying for my education, nor do we have anything like a GI bill to pass along. The goal is to provide them with guidance to help them get funding, but teaching them how not to make the same mistakes I did. I will encourage our girls to attend a public state college and to work part-time to assist with their college expenses. Applying for scholarships and grants is a must as well. I also learned about the great benefit of a 529 plan for kids. A 529 plan is a **tax-advantaged savings plan designed to encourage saving for future college costs**. These are sponsored by states, state agencies, or educational institutions and are authorized by Section 529 of the Internal Revenue Code. It is a great way to start a savings fund for Arianna since she still in elementary school.

## Helping Others While Helping Yourself

One of the disadvantages to living in Florida while trying to get out of a financial crisis has been the notion that our house is where all our family should come when they go on vacation. One year, we had family at our home for their vacation every single month! I love my family, but I had to put a stop to it. I decided to give notice to everyone via social media. I advised that my house would not be available during certain months of the year. The only exception was for our parents. They were always welcome. It just wasn't fair for others to assume that they could save on their travel expenses by staying with us. We were in the midst of getting our finances in order and having visitors often affected that because there were expenses associated with having extra guests in the house. Between making sure we had fresh linens, to buying groceries to make sure there was food for everyone, it was a lot of pressure. At one point, we even considered getting an SUV that could accommodate seven to eight passengers so it could be available when the family came to visit. Wrong! The reality is that we were not responsible for making that kind of accommodation. I have been blessed to be hospitable, and we enjoyed our family, but we had our commitments and goals on which we needed to focus. Yes, we loved having our family over, and we took pride in being generous, but we sometimes had to say no for the sake of keeping our own house in order. The journey to financial freedom has at times been lonely, but to live in the abundance that we were seeking, we needed to stay on track to level up and grow so we could give back to our family and the Hispanic community.

As business owners, sometimes family and friends don't understand what it takes to run a business or the financial stress we go through when business is slow. Between working more hours than what you work on a traditional job to cutting back on hanging out, it requires a lot. As a business owner, you have to consider the number of clients you have so you can gauge what your income is going to be. You have to be aware of the work you have lined up so that you can afford the rent, utilities, or food for the family. Many people don't understand, especially those who get resources such as government benefits. Most of the time, we were not considered a low-income family, so we had to work hard to make ends meet because we didn't qualify for those same government benefits. There were those around us who didn't understand what that was like. We didn't get Medicaid, so we had an insurance plan with a very high deductible, and there was even a time when we didn't have any medical insurance at all. It was frustrating dealing with those who thought we should live a certain way, without considering all that we had going on.

I was discouraged at realizing how much I had to go through to learn how to be fiscally responsible. The concepts of how to manage money was not a topic that was discussed as I was growing up. One of the only things I heard people in my family talk about was the expensive things they bought on large credit lines, or how they had 0% financing. I had spent years admiring people for what they had, only to realize they went into debt to have those things. Not to mention being surrounded by family or friends who worked for the government. Their well-deserved benefits are incredible, but at the same time we couldn't get answers from them on how to get great benefits in other career paths because the only solution they had was "working for the government" or "join the armed forces."

## Networking and Finding Answers

My husband started a side hustle making online sales after we relaunched our business. Sales were slow in the beginning but did very well the following year. The goal of this venture was to pay off my student loans and save for future investments. I also found a great opportunity in real estate. I found a coach online and decided to get some paid training. I joined a local Real Estate Investor Association or REIA, which was a blessed opportunity. This organization was full of like-minded individuals who were passionate about creating wealth. We were recommended to read the book *Rich Dad, Poor Dad* by Robert Kiyosaki. I had previously read this book but felt the need to revisit the text. I realized that I identified with Mr. Kiyosaki a lot. He had even joined the military but didn't retire from it, and still lived a successful life.

Many of the members of the REIA were interested in my husband's business. As a result of this, we upgraded our membership from individual to business, and we gained more clients. Being a part of this organization opened many doors in addition to our being able to increase our knowledge of the Real Estate Industry. It was great networking with others who could benefit from our small business. Finally, I felt I was surrounded by people that I could identify with. They were able to provide me with answers to the many questions I had regarding business and finance.

After six months of being a part of the organization, we acquired our first investment property. We were able to buy, rehabilitate, and rent the property within three months, all while working our jobs, handling the kids and other business responsibilities. I was ecstatic to share with others our experience as new real estate investors. Real estate became a great passion for me because I had experienced what it is to be homeless. It was an honor and pleasure to become a landlord and provide affordable housing within our community.

## Blaming Others

There was a time when I blamed my parents for not teaching me about personal finance. I was disappointed that they didn't pay for my college education and the fact that I didn't inherit anything when my dad passed away. I was upset with the government about the Great Recession, although I was responsible for the student loans I had. The reality is that I had to grow up and stop blaming others. When you stop blaming others, you start seeing things differently. You must take responsibility for your own life and every single step you take. Everything you go through has a meaningful purpose for you. It is easy to fall into the trap of believing that your opportunities are limited because of your accent, skin color or heritage. You must put all excuses aside and decide to work as hard as necessary to accomplish what you want in life.

## Frugality & Creativity

One of the ways we cut costs as we were getting our financial lives in order was buying our furniture from platforms such as Offer up, Craigslist, and Facebook Market Place. We repurposed items to create decor that gave our home the feel of a farmhouse. Do-it-yourself projects can be so fulfilling. The creativity you use allows you to create the look and feel you desire, all while cutting costs. This also taught me how to enjoy what I have. We don't buy new furniture then feel the need to "upgrade." We turn those opportunities into family projects. We love thrift shopping as well and enjoy the savings we get on great clothing.

## Goal Setting

As I was meditating one day, I realized that I always had an unending list of goals I wanted to accomplish in life. Each time I reached a goal, I had another to follow. At one point, I wasn't sure whether this was a good or bad thing, but honestly, it contributed to getting me where I am today. One of my goals has been to become the proud CEO of my life, create my own "economy" and be a person of value in this world. My personal goals inspire me and allow me to aspire to those higher things. I love seeing others succeed as well, and as a working woman with a family, it feels great to see others do great because I know the struggle. Setting goals has been of great benefit to me.

## When Will I Stop?

I will never stop improving. I have become so passionate about life, and I wake up every day knowing that there are many opportunities to pursue. I encourage you to do the same. I'm grateful to live in a country where there are so many possibilities. On the other hand, I have come to a point in my life where I am content with what I have and who I have become. I enjoy more experiences than things, and I don't need the new model of anything to be fulfilled. I no longer compare myself to others or hold myself to unreasonable standards. I have shifted my focus to helping others, not as a financial guru but as a financial literacy contributor.

Although I am not Oprah, Jennifer Lopez, or Olga Tanon, I continuously move forward. I learned to stop looking at celebrities and seeing the "celebrity," but to see entrepreneurship. Like any business, they need to have a target audience, be likable and build their brand. Many celebrities have ventures such as clothing lines, magazines, become brand ambassadors for other businesses, or own stocks and real estate. They come to a point where they generate income without sweating their butts off on stage or creating content. They are not like the average person who generates income by working for others then spend every single dime. Average people, who at the beginning of the year, see their W2 and wonder where all the money went. In other words, we only focus on earned income, which is the money that you earn by doing something or by trading your time for money, e.g., the money that you make on your job. Others that are more financially savvy invest to generate passive or active income such as profit, interest, dividend, rental, royalty income or Capital Gains.

Take charge of your life and be intentional with your money. Know where every dime is going by tracking your expenses and avoid overspending. There are many apps out there to utilize for this.

# Keys I Use to Improve My Life

Here is a series of steps to take, along with suggestions to get out of a financial mess. Start with prayer, and continuously pray for wisdom and guidance.

**Generate Income**

➢ Get a job and/or start a business.

**Money Mindset**

➢ Stop Instant gratification and start thinking for the future.

**Manage Finances**

> ➤ Start a budget.
> ➤ Payoff debt.
> ➤ Downsize if necessary.

**Invest In Yourself**

> ➤ Get a journal and create a vision board.
> ➤ Increase Savings.
> ➤ Continue self-education, personal, and professional development.
> ➤ Hire mentors or coaches.
> ➤ Surround yourself with like-minded people, find your tribe, go to Networking events or groups, Tradeshows, Meetup Groups, Facebook Communities, and mastermind groups.

**Create Wealth**

> ➤ Get assets instead of liabilities.
> ➤ Put money to work for you: ***Invest!***

**Give Back**

> ➤ Tithe.
> ➤ Volunteer.
> ➤ Go on missions trips.
> ➤ Open a Non-Profit Organization.

Remember, it is not how much you make that determines your success, but how well you are using your resources to improve your quality of life. I wish I knew these things in my 20's, but there is always time to start a new journey. I heard stories from people beginning this journey as early as in their teen years to as late as their 60's. Why should you live your life watching others thrive? Refuse to keep watching others chase their dreams. Chase yours too! I believe in all of you, but you have to believe in yourself and do the work.

There is a saying, "When the student is ready, the teacher will appear." I have found this to be true. When I was ready to find answers, the resources came. Here is a summary of the lessons I learned along the way:

- ➢ **Have multiple streams of income.** This is important. Do not rely solely on your job for pay.
- ➢ **Learn new skills.** This will open new doors and opportunities to generate more income.
- ➢ **Think long-term.** It can be challenging to let go of instant gratification, but it is worth it. If you have become comfortable with your life and everything is "convenient," you may be doing things wrong. Consider the long-term effects of your decisions.
- ➢ **Read**. There are so many books out there that have the answers I had been looking for all these years. You can save yourself a lot of time and energy by increasing your knowledge through reading.

Some of the books I read to find some guidance were:

1. *Total Money Makeover* by Dave Ramsey
2. *Love Your Life Not Theirs* by Rachel Cruze

3. *Your Money or Your Life* by Vicky Robins
4. *The Millionaire Next Door* by William D. Danko, Thomas J. Stanley
5. *Rich Dad Poor Dad* by Robert Kiyosaki


We also completed Financial Peace University by Dave Ramsey and attended his Smart Money Tours for debt payoff.

# Final Thoughts

I have had many jobs during my life to make ends meet, but I was intentional about getting to the point of doing the things for which I am passionate. Why should you stay at a job that you don't like for 20-30 years? You must genuinely enjoy it if you are going to remain on a job for that length of time. Find something you love to do and work on it after your regular job hours or on your days off. You never know whether your passion will turn into profits and eventually become your primary business or career. Don't waste time if you want to build your brand or business. Get on it and think big!

I have surrounded myself with like-minded people by going to networking events, conferences or joining meetups, Facebook or mastermind groups. That has honestly worked for me. It is imperative to find a tribe that will celebrate your wins. Not everyone in your circle will celebrate your accomplishments. Pay close attention and don't feel obligated to share everything with everyone. It is best to avoid any negativity from family, friends or from social media to keep moving forward. Surrounding myself with people who were not on the same path as I affected my productivity. I decided to change that. As a result, a beautiful new world of opportunities opened up for me. Remember, entrepreneurship is not always celebrated, and that is fine. Most people believe getting a government job is better, but it's ok if you determine that it is not for you.

You must be willing to come outside of your comfort zone to start achieving new goals and develop and grow your professional life. Your future does not have to be like your past. Understand that you are responsible for your life and you must keep moving forward. Ask God for direction, create a plan from your vision, write it down and take action! Always ask yourself what you're doing today to help you achieve your goals. Take monthly assessments to track your progress. You will see your life take a significant turn.

Maybe you have a nine to five, and you are desperate to leave. I understand that feeling. Use that as motivation to get your financial situation in order. Whenever I have come to the point of disliking a job or become unsure of the stability of that job, I take the time to assess my skills so that I can increase my chances of moving forward and creating a better opportunity for myself. Sometimes it was finding a better job. Other times I created income from a side hustle. Be aware of this so you can generate money to save, invest and gain the ability to say goodbye to that job.

I decided to share my story because there is no greater joy than to reach those who have never planned for their future as a result of not having the knowledge, tools or resources. My past experiences have had a tremendous impact on my journey. My struggles have equipped me to learn more than I ever knew concerning finances. Learning that you do not need to be a government employee, a millionaire celebrity, or a lotto winner to have a bright financial future opened a whole new world of possibilities for me. My husband and I decided that entrepreneurship was the way to go and we don't regret that decision. Yes, we work more hours than the average 40 hour work week, but having a flexible schedule is priceless. We go to the kid's activities at school, attend conferences, enjoy beach days during the week, go on vacation for weeks instead of days, and are able to help others in the process. Building a life that you don't need a vacation from is what financial freedom is all about and I would love for everyone to have the ability to work towards having that great life.

# How to reach me

I would love for you to share your financial freedom journey with me, your struggles and any other topics you would like to cover regarding becoming financially free. Please email me at info@darlenenunezllc.com. I want to hear how you, my amazing readers, are doing! Feel free to visit my website at www.darlenenunezllc.com.